REC

SPACE DISCOVERY GUIDES

PRIVATE
SPACE TRAVEL

A SPACE DISCOVERY GUIDE

Margaret J. Goldstein

Lerner Publications ◆ Minneapolis

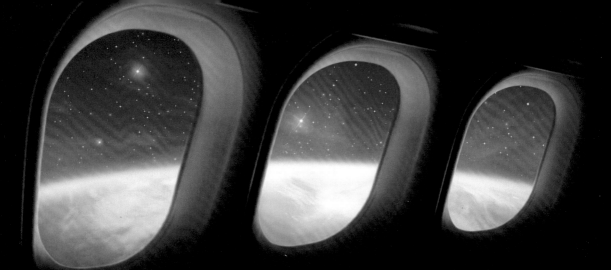

Lerner Publications Company
A division of Lerner Publishing Group, Inc.
241 First Avenue North
Minneapolis, MN 55401 USA

For reading levels and more information, look up this title at www.lernerbooks.com.

Main body text set in Avenir LT Std 65 Medium 11.5/17.5.
Typeface provided by Adobe Systems.

Library of Congress Cataloging-in-Publication Data

Names: Goldstein, Margaret J.
Title: Private space travel: a space discovery guide / Margaret J. Goldstein.
Description: Minneapolis : Lerner Publications, [2017] | Series: Space
    discovery guides | Audience: Age 9–12. | Audience: Grade 4 to 6. |
    Includes bibliographical references and index.
Identifiers: LCCN 2016018647 (print) | LCCN 2016019479 (ebook) |
    ISBN 9781512425895 (lb : alk. paper) | ISBN 9781512427974 (eb pdf)
Subjects: LCSH: Space tourism—Juvenile literature. | Manned space
    flight—Juvenile literature.
Classification: LCC TL793 .G6285 2017 (print) | LCC TL793 (ebook) | DDC
    910.919—dc23

LC record available at https://lccn.loc.gov/2016018647

Manufactured in the United States of America
1-41357-23301-7/7/2016

TABLE OF CONTENTS

INTRODUCTION
A STAR-STUDDED DEBUT

Richard Branson introduces Virgin Galactic's new spacecraft, *Unity*.

The air was electric inside a big hangar (aircraft shed) at the Mojave Air and Space Port in Southern California. Music pounded, and a crowd of people flocked to a stage beneath dazzling blue lights. Something exciting was about to happen.

The date was February 19, 2016, and Virgin Galactic, a pioneering space tourism company, was about to unveil its newest spaceship, *Unity*. To loud applause, a white Range Rover drove onto the stage with the sleek and shiny spacecraft in tow. Virgin Galactic founder Richard Branson, a British businessman, proudly introduced *Unity* to the crowd.

Harrison Ford attends the unveiling of *Unity (inset)*. A crowd gathers to get a closer look at *Unity (below)*.

The gathering was a star-studded event. Actor Harrison Ford, who played Han Solo in four *Star Wars* movies, was there. Malala Yousafzai, who had earned worldwide honors for fighting for the rights of girls in her native Pakistan, praised the new spaceship in a video shown at the event. "It's such a great work," she said. "And it's a way that we are inspiring young people in this whole world to explore more, to go farther and to have no boundaries."

The most moving words came from British physicist Stephen Hawking. He did not attend the event but spoke to the crowd through a recording. "We are entering a new space age," Hawking said. "Taking more and more passengers out into space will enable them and us [humankind] to look both outwards and back, but with a fresh perspective in both directions. It will help bring new meaning to our place on Earth and to our

Stephen Hawking sent a recorded speech to the Virgin Galactic event. He is excited about the future of space travel for humanity.

responsibilities as its stewards, and it will help us to recognize our place and our future in the cosmos—which is where I believe our ultimate destiny lies."

Hawking is one of around seven hundred people with tickets to ride on *Unity* when it's ready to fly. The craft will take six passengers at a time for a short ride into space.

Several other firms are also gearing up to fly tourists into space. Before the twenty-first century, only trained astronauts could travel into space and only government agencies operated spacecraft. As of 2016, only about 550 people had visited the vast expanse beyond Earth. But private businesses are jumping into the space travel industry. They will open the experience of spaceflight to thousands of tourists from nations around the world.

Aboard *Unity* and other vehicles, space tourists will experience several minutes of weightlessness—the feeling of being free of the pull of Earth's gravity. They will also get spectacular views of Earth from space. The rides won't come cheap, though. A flight on *Unity* costs about $250,000. But many people think it's a fair price to pay for the trip of a lifetime.

Very few people have seen Earth from space. This image was created by combining several satellite images.

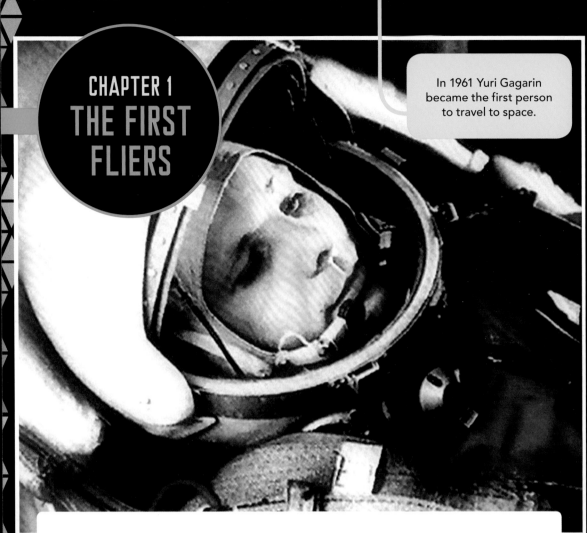

CHAPTER 1
THE FIRST FLIERS

In 1961 Yuri Gagarin became the first person to travel to space.

The first human to go to space was Yuri Gagarin, an air force pilot from the Soviet Union, a nation based in Russia from 1922 to 1991. In 1961 Gagarin orbited, or circled, Earth in a spaceship called *Vostok I*. During this era, people were eager to explore space. They wanted to learn more about the moon, the sun, and the rest of the solar system. They wanted to launch satellites that could photograph and study Earth from space, relay communications signals, and assist military operations. The Soviet Union and the United States raced to outdo each other in space technology.

The Soviet Union scored the first victory in the "space race" when it sent an unpiloted craft into orbit in 1957. The United States sent its own craft into orbit the next year. Yuri Gagarin's groundbreaking 1961 voyage showed that human space travel was possible. After Gagarin's trip, many more astronauts traveled into space. Some only orbited Earth as Gagarin did. Others visited the moon. Many astronauts flew to orbiting laboratories such as the Mir Space Station and the International Space Station (ISS).

All these travelers worked for government space agencies. Their missions were mostly scientific. For instance, astronauts visiting the moon brought back moon rocks for study by scientists on

This moon rock was collected by *Apollo 12* astronauts.

Earth. The ISS is an orbiting research laboratory. Astronauts there carry out many experiments. In one experiment, they study how microscopic life-forms grow and change in space. Astronauts also take part in medical tests on the ISS. The tests help doctors learn how weightlessness affects the human body.

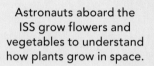

Astronauts aboard the ISS grow flowers and vegetables to understand how plants grow in space.

This astronaut works on the ISS to study how weightlessness affects cells in the immune system.

Dennis Tito (left) and two Russian astronauts pose aboard the ISS during the first space tourism trip (above). A Soyuz rocket blasts off to take Tito to the ISS (right).

▶ A $20 MILLION TRIP

In 2001 Dennis Tito, a wealthy California businessman, became the first space tourist. A former engineer with the US National Aeronautics and Space Administration (NASA), Tito had dreamed of flying into space since he was a teenager. NASA opposed sending tourists into space because they were not trained to operate spacecraft or to deal with emergencies in space. But the Russian government saw an opportunity to make money by taking tourists to space. Russia agreed to fly Tito to the ISS for $20 million. He spent about eight hundred hours training with the Russian space agency before the trip.

Anousheh Ansari, an Iranian American businesswoman, became the first female space tourist when she visited the ISS in 2006.

On April 28, 2001, Tito lifted off in a Soyuz capsule with two Russian astronauts. He spent six days on the space station before returning to Earth. Since Tito's trip, six other space tourists have taken Soyuz capsules to visit the ISS.

THE X PRIZE

Private aerospace businesses work with governments to design and build spacecraft. But private space travel, with no government involvement, used to be off-limits. Before 2004 private space travel was against the law in the United States. And it costs billions of dollars to build and launch piloted space vehicles. This is too costly for most private companies. Government space agencies can afford to fund space expeditions. They do so not to make a profit but to advance scientific knowledge.

In the late twentieth century, US businessman Peter Diamandis envisioned a future for private space travel. He was inspired by aviation pioneer Charles Lindbergh's 1927 nonstop flight across the Atlantic Ocean. A wealthy hotel owner had offered $25,000 to the first pilot to make the trip. Lindbergh won the prize in his plane *Spirit of St. Louis*. In 1996 Diamandis formed an organization called the New Spirit of St. Louis. He offered a $10 million prize to the first nongovernment team to build a reusable space vehicle. To win the contest, called the X Prize (later the Ansari X Prize), the vehicle would have to carry three people to a height of at least 62 miles (100 kilometers) above Earth. At about this point, the atmosphere (the layer of gases surrounding the planet) ends and space begins. To show that the craft was reusable, the winning team would have to make the round-trip flight twice in two weeks.

Peter Diamandis speaks at an X Prize meeting in 2013.

Twenty-six teams entered the competition. One of them was called Mojave Aerospace Ventures. The team was led by US aircraft designer Burt Rutan and his company, Scaled Composites. Microsoft cofounder Paul Allen provided financial support to the team. To capture the prize, the team built a craft called SpaceShipOne. Its design was unique. It didn't blast off from the ground like a typical spacecraft. Instead, a double-hulled airplane called White Knight carried SpaceShipOne and its crew into the sky. At about 9.5 miles (15 km) above Earth, White Knight released SpaceShipOne. It immediately fired its rocket engines and shot into space under its own power. After a few minutes in space, the ship headed back to Earth.

White Knight climbs into the air with SpaceShipOne attached.

The Ansari X Prize trophy was awarded to Mojave Aerospace Ventures in November 2004.

Left to right: Paul Allen, pilot Mike Melvill, and Burt Rutan stand together after SpaceShipOne's first flight.

SpaceShipOne made two successful trips in the fall of 2004, winning the $10 million prize for Mojave Aerospace Ventures.

OUT OF THIS WORLD

Branson was excited by the success of SpaceShipOne. He thought a similar craft could take tourists into space. He formed an aerospace company called Virgin Galactic and teamed with Scaled Composites to build a tourist ship. By then the United States had passed a new law allowing for private space travel.

People sit in the cabin of a SpaceShipTwo prototype in 2007.

Branson unveils Virgin Galactic's SpaceShipTwo at an air show in 2012.

Developing the new tourist vehicle, named SpaceShipTwo, took ten years. As news spread about upcoming tourist flights, hundreds of people made reservations with Virgin Galactic. The group included many celebrities, such as actors Brad Pitt, Angelina Jolie, Leonardo DiCaprio, Ashton Kutcher, and Tom Hanks, and pop stars Lady Gaga and Justin Bieber.

While readying the spaceship, tragedy struck. During a test flight in 2014, shortly after White Knight released SpaceShipTwo to begin its climb, a pilot pulled a lever in error. That mistake put the tail of the spacecraft into the wrong position. The ship pitched violently and broke apart in midair. One pilot parachuted to safety, but the other died as the craft fell apart.

About twenty SpaceShipTwo ticket holders canceled their reservations after the accident. But Virgin Galactic was determined to press ahead with space tourism. "We're going to learn what went wrong, discover how we can improve safety and performance, and then move forward together," Branson told reporters after the crash. "Most people in the world would love to see the dream [of space tourism] living on."

Sheriff's deputies inspect the wreckage of SpaceShipTwo after it crashed in 2014.

CHAPTER 2
THE TOP TOURS

This artist's concept shows a planned spaceport on an island in the Caribbean.

In the second decade of the twenty-first century, private space travel is a growing industry. Many private companies are drawing up plans for space cargo ships, launch vehicles, probes, landing craft, spaceports, and even human space habitats. Only time will tell which businesses will succeed.

But by far the most exciting space travel companies are those offering space rides to paying tourists. No space tourist businesses are yet ready to fly, but they all promise a thrilling ride.

Branson speaks to a crowd gathered to witness the unveiling of *Unity*.

VIRGIN GALACTIC

After the 2014 SpaceShipTwo disaster, Virgin Galactic built a new, safer version of its spaceship and renamed it *Unity*. This is the ship Branson introduced to the world in February 2016. At 60 feet (18 meters) long, *Unity* is about four times longer than a sports utility vehicle. The cockpit seats two pilots. The passenger cabin holds six seats—three on each side of a central aisle.

On flights in *Unity*, passengers will wear padded helmets and flight suits. They'll be strapped into their seats before takeoff. At first the voyage will feel somewhat like an ordinary airplane flight. Taking off from a runway at Spaceport America in New Mexico, White Knight will carry *Unity* high into the sky. After about forty-five minutes, White Knight will release *Unity* to fly alone. The ship will fire its rockets and zoom toward space.

At the edge of space, the pilot will shut off *Unity*'s engines. All of a sudden, passengers will feel weightlessness, also called zero gravity. They will be able to unbuckle their seat straps and float through *Unity*'s cabin for about four minutes. Through *Unity*'s windows, passengers will see Earth curving beneath them. They will see the sun, stars, and planets moving through the vast blackness of space.

Passengers will strap in again for the trip back to Earth. On the way down, the ship will first dive through the atmosphere and then glide like an airplane back to Spaceport America. The whole journey, from start to finish, will last about an hour and a half.

BLUE ORIGIN

A company called Blue Origin, headed by Jeff Bezos, the founder of Amazon.com, also promises breathtaking rides into space. The company website draws in passengers with the following: "From arrival at our desert launch site to the heart-pounding emotions at launch to

Jeff Bezos stands by *New Shepard* before its first launch.

weightlessness and perfect stillness of space—be a pioneer in the next era of human spaceflight." Blue Origin passengers will begin their journey at a spaceport in West Texas. Dressed in flight suits, six passengers will enter a crew capsule atop a 60-foot-tall (18 m) rocket called *New Shepard*. The passengers will strap in, and the rocket and crew capsule will blast into the sky.

Passengers on Blue Origin flights will sit in a capsule on top of a powerful rocket.

As it nears the top of the atmosphere, *New Shepard* will release the crew capsule. While the rocket falls back to Earth, the capsule will continue to climb on its own. When it reaches the edge of space, passengers will unbuckle their safety straps and float weightlessly. Inside the capsule, they'll have enough room to turn somersaults. They'll take in spectacular views of Earth and space through large windows.

Passengers will strap back into their seats for the return to Earth. Rockets and three parachutes will slow the craft as it falls through the atmosphere. The capsule will make a soft landing only a few miles from its launch site.

Blue Origin plans to begin its tourist flights in 2018. The company has not yet announced how much it will cost to ride *New Shepard* into space.

A *New Shepard* rocket lands vertically after launching into space.

Reusable Rockets

Most space vehicles, such as those that travel to the ISS, reach space with the help of rockets. Rockets give spacecraft the speed they need to overcome the pull of Earth's gravity. Once a craft is traveling fast enough to beak away from this pull, rockets are no longer needed. They separate from a spacecraft and fall back toward Earth. Falling rockets usually break apart high in the atmosphere or smash up when they hit the ground. Old rockets can't be reused. Space agencies need brand-new rockets to launch new spacecraft.

Spaceflight would be much less expensive if rockets were reusable, so for many years, aerospace engineers have tried to develop reusable rockets. Blue Origin has finally achieved that goal. The company's *New Shepard* space vehicle consists of a passenger capsule and a reusable rocket. The rocket blasts the capsule high into the atmosphere. After the two sections of the spacecraft separate, the rocket portion drops back to Earth. As it falls, it remains in a straight up-and-down position. When it nears the ground, its engines power up to slow its fall. Then it gently lands on four legs.

Another aerospace company, SpaceX, is also building reusable rockets. The company's visionary leader is Elon Musk, who also founded the Internet financial services business PayPal and the electric car company Tesla Motors. SpaceX's reusable rockets, named Falcons, are being used to launch NASA vehicles to the ISS. Because they send spacecraft far beyond Earth's atmosphere, Falcons are much more powerful than *New Shepard* rockets. On April 8, 2016, a Falcon rocket launched a NASA cargo vehicle into space from Cape Canaveral in Florida. After the cargo vehicle and the rocket separated, the rocket fell back to Earth and landed upright on a barge in the Atlantic Ocean. This was the first successful landing for a Falcon.

SpaceX successfully lands its Falcon rocket on a barge in the Atlantic Ocean.

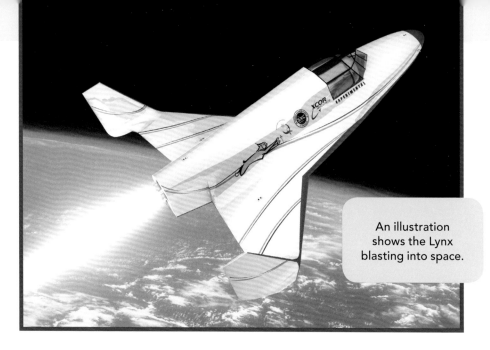

An illustration shows the Lynx blasting into space.

XCOR AEROSPACE

Texas-based XCOR Aerospace plans to take passengers into space in a rocket plane called Lynx. The vehicle takes off and lands like an airplane. It is a two-seat craft, with room for one pilot and one passenger. The two will sit side by side during the trip into space.

XCOR tests Lynx engines in Mojave, California.

The plane will shoot into the sky like a bullet. It will take less than five minutes for Lynx to reach the edge of space. There the pilot will shut down the plane's engines, and the passenger can float weightlessly for about five minutes. The cockpit's big wraparound window will offer breathtaking views of Earth and space.

For the return trip, the plane will rocket back into the atmosphere and then slow down to glide gently to the ground. The whole trip will take less than forty-five minutes.

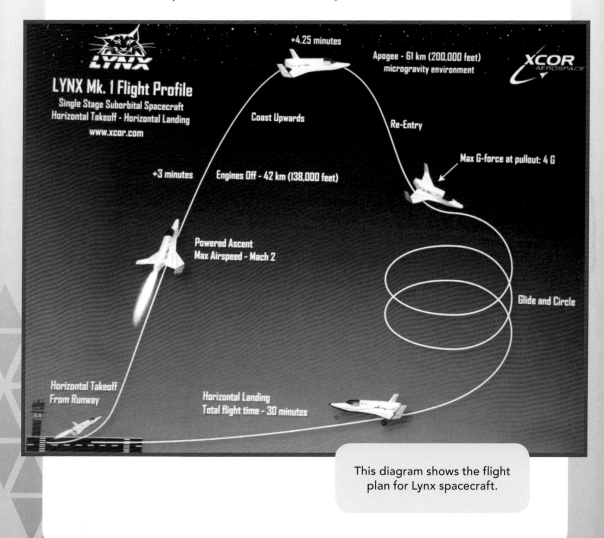

This diagram shows the flight plan for Lynx spacecraft.

After the passenger deplanes, the XCOR crew will prepare for another passenger and another flight. XCOR expects to make up to four passenger flights per day. The company has started selling tickets, which cost $150,000 each. XCOR hasn't said when flights will begin, but more than three hundred people have already made reservations.

WORLD VIEW ENTERPRISES

World View Enterprises won't fly passengers as high as the other space tourism companies, but it offers a thrilling ride nevertheless. The Arizona-based business will take passengers aloft in a capsule suspended beneath a parafoil and a helium balloon. The capsule has room for two pilots and six passengers.

The craft will launch from Spaceport Tucson in Arizona. It will travel slowly, only about 11 miles (18 km) per hour. In about

This artist's image shows the World View Enterprises capsule, parafoil, and balloon floating at the edge of space.

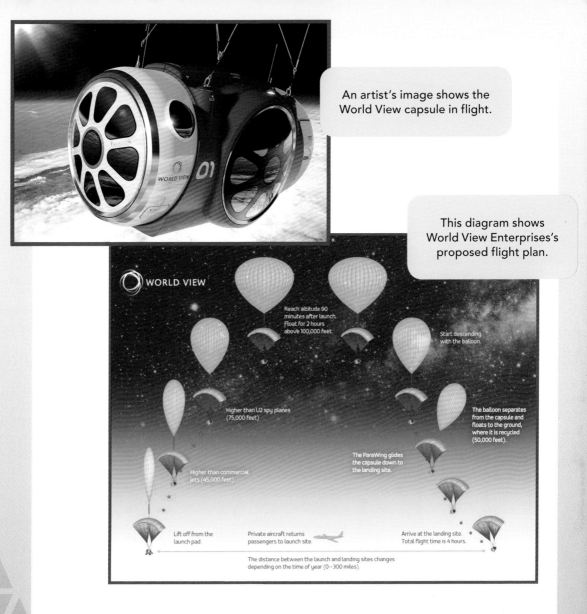

An artist's image shows the World View capsule in flight.

This diagram shows World View Enterprises's proposed flight plan.

WORLD VIEW

Reach altitude 90 minutes after launch. Float for 2 hours above 100,000 feet.

Start descending with the balloon.

Higher than U2 spy planes (75,000 feet)

The balloon separates from the capsule and floats to the ground, where it is recycled (50,000 feet).

The ParaWing glides the capsule down to the landing site.

Higher than commercial jets (45,000 feet).

Lift off from the launch pad.

Private aircraft returns passengers to launch site.

Arrive at the landing site. Total flight time is 4 hours.

The distance between the launch and landing sites changes depending on the time of year (0–300 miles).

two hours, the craft will reach an altitude of 19 miles (30 km)—a level known as near space. At this height, the views are just as astonishing as they are higher up.

Passengers won't experience weightlessness on a World View ride, but they will enjoy a gentle five-hour round-trip. They'll need to buckle into their seats only during takeoff and landing. Otherwise, they can walk freely through the capsule, which

This illustration shows passengers viewing space from the World View Enterprises capsule.

contains a bathroom and even a refreshment bar. Through big bubble windows, passengers will see Earth stretching out below them and space above. The pilots will point out celestial objects such as stars and planets.

After two hours in near space, the craft will head back to Earth. On the way down, the helium balloon and the parafoil will separate. Then the parafoil will act like a parachute, lowering the

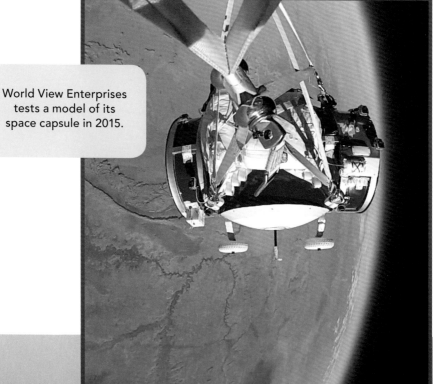

World View Enterprises tests a model of its space capsule in 2015.

tour capsule gently to the ground. Depending on the strength and direction of the winds, the capsule might touch down several hundred miles from Spaceport Tucson. The company will fly passengers back to Tucson in a private plane.

The price for a World View flight is $75,000. The company hopes to launch its first flights in 2017.

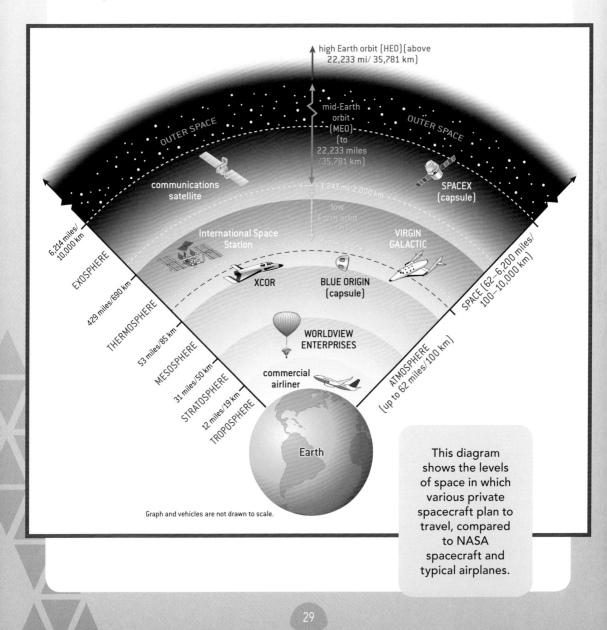

Graph and vehicles are not drawn to scale.

This diagram shows the levels of space in which various private spacecraft plan to travel, compared to NASA spacecraft and typical airplanes.

CHAPTER 3
A ROUGH RIDE

Rockets must be incredibly powerful to break free of the pull of Earth's gravity.

Flying into space and floating in zero gravity sounds like a blast. But space tourists should know that a trip through Earth's atmosphere can be a physically punishing ride. Rockets travel at supersonic speeds. The Lynx, for instance, hits a top speed of Mach 2.9—or 2,208 miles (3,553 km) per hour—nearly three times faster than the speed of sound. *Unity*, *New Shepard*, and other rocket-powered tourist vehicles will go just as fast. Vehicles traveling that fast shake and vibrate, which means that the travelers inside them shake and vibrate too. The roar of the rocket engines can be deafening.

Doctors monitor Italian astronaut Samantha Cristoforetti as she experiences high g-forces during a training session.

HIGH Gs

Accelerating and decelerating (speeding up and slowing down) at extremely high speeds increases the force of gravity pushing against a person's body. For example, when *Unity* rockets upward after being released by White Knight, passengers will feel up to 3 g-forces (or 3 Gs) pressing against their chests. That's three times the force gravity normally exerts on the body. The pressure can make it difficult to breathe. Some people might even black out during the experience. The g-forces will climb even higher during the trip back to Earth. The return trip on Lynx will subject the pilot and passenger to 4 g-forces. As the company's website explains, "[These g-forces last] only 20 seconds but truly [it's] not a picnic."

Weightlessness, or zero gravity, does not punish the body the way high g-forces do. But weightlessness can confuse the inner ear, the organ that control's balance. So astronauts often become nauseated and vomit when they enter zero gravity. The same thing might happen to passengers on space tours, although taking antinausea medicine ahead of time can help.

Unity uses an innovative tail design to achieve a smoother descent.

Belly Flop

Returning to Earth from space can be more difficult than blasting off. Spaceships speeding into the atmosphere are hard for pilots to control. And at supersonic speeds, plummeting spacecraft grow extremely hot as they rub against gases in the air. Most space vehicles are protected by heat shields, which keep them from burning up and breaking apart as they descend.

Scaled Composites built SpaceShipOne with an innovative system to make a descent through the atmosphere slower, cooler, and more stable. *Unity* uses the same design. The spaceship has a hinged twin tail that can be raised to a 60-degree angle. When the ship is climbing or flying straight, the tail sits level with the vehicle. But for reentering the atmosphere, the tail moves all the way up. Raising the tail causes the plane to descend flat on its belly—as though it's doing a belly flop. This position slows the craft and makes it more stable as it falls. Because the descent is slow, heat shields aren't needed. At about 70,000 feet (21,300 m) above Earth, *Unity* pilots will drop the tail back to its level position and the craft will glide to Earth like an airplane.

PREPARING PASSENGERS

Before sending passengers on trips in rocket-powered vehicles, tour companies will put them through several days of training. Passengers will learn about their spaceships and how to maneuver inside them. They will also learn how to handle emergencies that might arise during a trip.

Astronauts complete many medical and emergency training exercises before traveling to the ISS. Many space tourists will also have to train for emergencies.

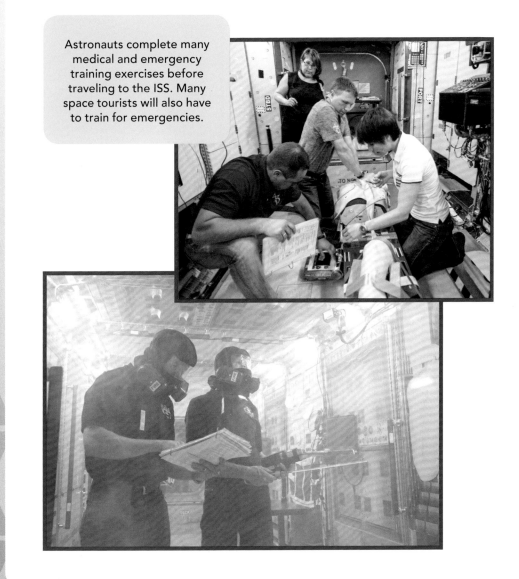

Part of the training will include time in a spinning machine called a human centrifuge. As the centrifuge spins, the person inside feels high g-forces, equal to what passengers will experience in real spaceflight. Before entering the centrifuge, space tourists will learn how to breathe more easily at high Gs by taking short and shallow breaths. They can practice this technique in the centrifuge. Other training machines will give riders a feeling of being weightless.

An astronaut experiences weightlessness as part of his training *(top)*. A human centrifuge machine is used to train astronauts to deal with high g-forces *(bottom)*.

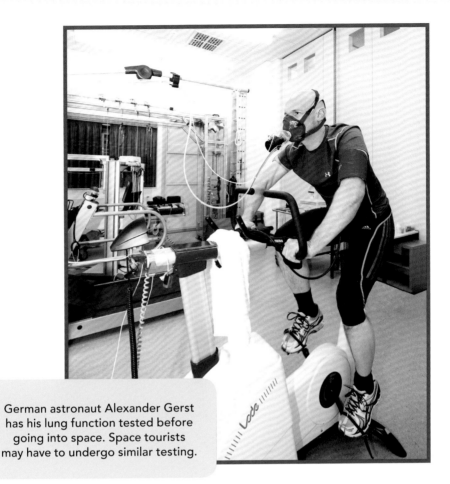

German astronaut Alexander Gerst has his lung function tested before going into space. Space tourists may have to undergo similar testing.

Tour companies will administer medical tests to make sure passengers are healthy enough to fly in space. Those who have serious health problems, such as heart disease, might not be allowed to take the trip.

The only company that won't put passengers through testing and training is World View. Traveling slowly through the atmosphere beneath a balloon does not create high g-forces going up or down. And since World View passengers won't experience weightlessness, they won't need to prepare with zero gravity machines or take antinausea medication.

A Virgin Galactic hangar in New Mexico

Space tourism businesses need more than just rockets and spaceships. They also need spaceports where craft can blast off and land. They need teams of trained pilots, mechanics, and other staff members. Tour companies must also make sure that their vehicles don't interfere with or harm airplane traffic, other space traffic, or people on the ground. They need safety rules and regulations.

White Knight (*above*) and SpaceShipOne took off and landed at the Mojave Air and Space Port during its test flights.

SPACEPORTS

Across the United States, several spaceports are ready for business, and more will be built as the space tourism industry grows. Aerospace companies have been testing military and civilian aircraft at California's Mojave Air and Space Port since World War II (1939–1945). In the first decade of the twenty-first century, SpaceShipOne made its test flights from Mojave. XCOR, Virgin Galactic, and other aerospace companies have also test-flown vehicles there.

The wide-open California desert, home to the Mojave Air and Space Port, is a popular place for companies to build and test spacecraft.

In the 2010s, the state of New Mexico built Spaceport America to serve Virgin Galactic and other space tourism businesses. Located in a desert called the Jornada del Muerto in southern New Mexico, the spaceport has a runway, a hangar, training facilities, and a terminal. It is ready for flights as soon as Virgin Galactic is ready to launch *Unity*.

Spaceport Tucson is under construction in Arizona. World View Enterprises will operate the site and launch its tourist balloons there. Arizona's Pima County owns the spaceport. Blue Origin owns and runs a private spaceport in Van Horn, Texas.

This illustration shows Spaceport Tucson, where World View Enterprises balloons will launch.

RULES OF THE ROAD

In the United States, the Federal Aviation Administration will make rules and regulations for the space tourism industry. It is drawing up guidelines for pilot training, safety procedures, and flight schedules. Only highly trained fighter pilots, test pilots, and astronauts will be licensed to fly space tourist vehicles.

But passengers need to know that no matter how many rules are in place, space travel is extremely risky. From 1981 to 2011, the United States operated a fleet of space shuttles. During those years, NASA estimated that the chance of a shuttle disaster was one in ninety. Indeed, fourteen astronauts have died in two space shuttle accidents, in 1986 and 2003. Space vehicle accidents have killed twenty-three astronauts and many more workers on the ground. Before they fly, space tourists will be required to sign documents stating that they understand the risks they take during a spaceflight.

NASA's space shuttle *Atlantis* launches in 2006. This was the first successful launch following the 2003 *Columbia* disaster, which killed all seven astronauts aboard the shuttle.

Even though no one can guarantee 100 percent safety for space travelers, rules and regulations are still important. Space tourism involves the entire planet, and nations need to work together to make the industry run smoothly. The aviation branch of the United Nations (UN), an international peacekeeping and humanitarian organization, wants space tourism regulations in place by 2019. The UN wants to make sure that businesses use the space around Earth wisely and as safely as possible.

Seven NASA astronauts were killed in 1986 when their shuttle broke apart seconds after launch *(top)*. The United Nations aviation branch is working to ensure that private space travel has regulations for safety *(left)*.

WHAT'S NEXT?

No one can say for sure where the space tourism industry is headed. But as tourist spaceflights become more common, the price of a ticket will probably fall. Space tourism will become accessible to more people, not just the extremely rich. And if the space tourist industry expands, it will provide thousands of jobs for spaceport workers and for spacecraft builders, mechanics, and pilots.

The spaceflights already in the works will carry people to the edge of space and back. The rides will be just for thrills. But Branson and others envision a time when spaceships will carry people from one part of Earth to another. On an airplane, it takes almost twenty-two hours to fly from London in the United Kingdom to Sydney, Australia. A space plane could make that journey in just a few hours. Saving so much time would be a great benefit to tourists and business travelers.

As space tourism becomes more common, new spacecraft will be designed and more people will have access to spaceflights.

Another destination for space tourists might be farther out in space at private, orbiting space hotels. Once tourists are able to orbit Earth, is the moon the next step for space tourism? What about Mars?

No one knows how far private space travel will go, but many people think it's a positive step for humanity. Blue Origin's Bezos says, "We should choose to go to space for many reasons. . . . But the one thing is, I think it's very inspiring for a certain kind of young kid to watch these missions, and it leads them to science, and engineering, and math. I think that's really good for the United States. I think it's really good for the world."

This artist's image shows what a future space hotel may look like.

Elon Musk hopes to send an uncrewed SpaceX spacecraft to Mars in 2018.

SpaceX's Elon Musk has even bigger dreams. He envisions colonies on Mars and other planets, and maybe even travel to other solar systems. He says, "If we're going to have any chance of sending stuff to other star systems, we need to be laser-focused on becoming a multi-planet civilization. That's the next step."

An artist's conception shows a future colony on Mars.

Source Notes

5   Mike Wall, "Virgin Galactic's New SpaceShipTwo Debut: Amid the Hoopla, Hope," *Space.com*, February 23, 2016, http://www.space.com/32009-virgin -galactic-spaceshiptwo-unveiling-party.html.

6   Mike Wall, "Stephen Hawking Wants to Ride Virgin Galactic's New Passenger Spaceship," *Space.com*, February 20, 2016, http://www.space.com/31993 -stephen-hawking-virgin-galactic-spaceshiptwo-unity.html.

17   CNNMoney staff, "Branson: The Dream of Space Tourism Lives On," *CNNMoney*, November 1, 2014, http://money.cnn.com/2014/11/01/news /companies/branson-virgin-space-tourism.

20   Jeff Bezos, quoted in Blue Origin, accessed May 6, 2016, https://www .blueorigin.com.

31   "The Spaceflight," XCOR, accessed May 6, 2016, http://spaceexpeditions .xcor.com/the-spaceflight.

42   Alan Boyle, "Jeff Bezos Lays Out Blue Origin's Space Vision, from Tourism to Off-Planet Heavy Industry," interview, GeekWire, April 13, 2016, http://www .geekwire.com/2016/interview-jeff-bezos.

43   Ross Andersen, "Exodus," Aeon, accessed May 6, 2016, https://aeon.co /essays/elon-musk-puts-his-case-for-a-multi-planet-civilisation.

Glossary

aerospace: a branch of science dealing with Earth's atmosphere and the space beyond it

altitude: height above Earth

astronaut: a person who pilots a spacecraft or works in space

atmosphere: a layer of gases surrounding a planet or another body in space

centrifuge: a machine that spins around at extremely high speeds. When a centrifuge accelerates, a person riding inside it feels high g-forces.

g-force: the force of gravity pushing against a person's body

gravity: a naturally occurring force that pulls objects in space toward one another. Gravity pulls objects near Earth toward the planet. In space, people do not feel the pull of Earth's gravity.

orbit: to travel around another object. The path an object takes during this trip is also called its orbit.

parafoil: a fabric object similar to a parachute that is able to be controlled and acts as an airplane wing in flight

rocket: an engine that pushes itself forward or upward by burning fuel. Unlike other kinds of engines, rockets do not draw in oxygen from the air. This feature enables them to operate in space.

supersonic: traveling faster than the speed of sound

weightlessness: freedom from the pull of gravity. People experience weightlessness when they leave Earth's atmosphere. Weightlessness is also called zero gravity.

Selected Bibliography

Associated Press. "Getting Lost in Space Will Soon Be How You Vacation." *New York Post*, February 15, 2016. http://nypost.com/2016/02/15/getting-lost-in -space-will-soon-be-how-you-vacation.

Chang, Kenneth. "Jeff Bezos Lifts Veil on His Rocket Company, Blue Origin." *New York Times*, March 8, 2016. http://www.nytimes.com/2016/03/09 /science/space/jeff-bezos-lifts-veil-on-his-rocket-company-blue-origin.html.

Langewiesche, William. "Everything You Need to Know about Flying Virgin Galactic." *Vanity Fair*, April 1, 2015. http://www.vanityfair.com /news/2015/03/what-is-it-like-to-fly-virgin-galactic.

Thompson, Kalee. "Your New Ride to Space." *Popular Science*, July 14, 2015. http://www.popsci.com/balloons-new-way-get-space.

Further Reading

Brake, Mark. *How to Be a Space Explorer: Your Out-of-This-World Adventure.* Oakland: Lonely Planet Kids, 2014.

Goodman, Susan E. *How Do You Burp in Space? And Other Tips Every Space Tourist Needs to Know.* New York: Bloomsbury, 2013.

Space Tourism for Kids 9–99
http://ontarioplanetarium.com/presentations/space-tourism-kids-9-99

Space Tourism in Science Fiction
http://www.spacefuture.com/tourism/sciencefiction.shtml

Space Tourism Society
http://spacetourismsociety.org

Waxman, Laura Hamilton. *Exploring Space Travel.* Minneapolis: Lerner Publications, 2012.

Index

Photo Acknowledgments

The images in this book are used with the permission of: © iStockphoto.com/narvikk, p. 2; AP Photo/Mark J. Terrill, pp. 4, 5 (top), 19; Gene Blevins/Polaris/Newscom, p. 5 (bottom); © Landmark-Media/ImageCollect, p. 6; NASA/Visible Earth, p. 7; © Heritage Image Partnership Ltd/Alamy, p. 8; NASA/Charles Conrad Jr, p. 9 (top); © Mark Williamson/Science Source, p. 9 (bottom); ESA/NASA, pp. 10 (both), 11 (left), 12; © Sovfoto/Universal Images Group/REX/Shutterstock, p. 11 (right); © XPRIZE Foundation/flickr.com (CC BY 2.0), p. 13; courtesy of Scaled Composites, LLC, pp. 14, 15 (left); AP Photo/James A. Finley, p. 15 (right); © REX/Shutterstock, p. 16 (left); © Daniel Berehulak/Getty Images, p. 16 (right); © Sandy Huffaker/Stringer/Getty Images, p. 17; XCOR media release, pp. 18, 24 (bottom); © Blue Origin, pp. 20, 21, 22, 30; courtesy of SpaceX, p. 23; PRNewswire/XCOR Aerospace, p. 24 (top); © Gabriel Bouys/AFP/Getty Images, p. 25; courtesy of World View Enterprises, Inc., pp. 26, 27 (both), 28 (both), 38; © Laura Westlund/Independent Picture Service, p. 29; GCTC, p. 31; © ZUMA Press/Alamy, p. 32; NASA/Bill Stafford, p. 33 (both); NASA, pp. 34 (top), 39, 40 (top); ESA/Kjetil Wormnes, p. 34 (bottom); ESA, p. 35; © Jim Thompson/Albuquerque Journal/ZUMAPRESS.com, p. 36; © Peter Brooker/REX/Shutterstock, p. 37 (top); © Leigh Green/Alamy, p. 37 (bottom); © iStockphoto.com/luca gavagna, p. 40 (bottom); © iStockphoto.com/Iurii Kovalenko, p. 41; © Victor Habbick Visions/Getty Images, p. 42; Mario Anzuoni/Reuters/Newscom, p. 43 (top); © Steven Hobbs/Stocktrek Images/Alamy, p. 43 (bottom).

Front cover: courtesy of SpaceX.